Estuarial

Wind in the Reeds

PUBLISHING

Walnut Creek, California

Published by Wind in the Reeds Publishing, 2015, 2018
1141 Bont Lane
Walnut Creek, CA 94596

ISBN 978-0-9897389-0-3
Second Edition.

For information about permission
to reproduce selections from this book, write to:

Jeff Reed
1141 Bont Lane Walnut Creek, CA 94596
(925) 708-1361 | windinthereedspub@gmail.com

Estuarial

Dedicated to Kelly Ballard

"We say that any two things however unlike are in something alike."

--Gerard Manley Hopkins
Notes on the *Spiritual Exercises*

Contents

Introduction

The title for this collection of poems *Estuarial* actually came out of a spiritual direction session with Dr. Susan Phillips when I was sharing with her how meaningful these poems had become to me. What she noticed, and what I instinctively loved about them, is how they bring (without manipulating a conclusion beforehand) two wildly disparate things together (like fresh water and sea water) and allow for a collision out of which rises up, instead of chaos and randomness, an intersection of common ground which bears witness to some kind of truth. The completion of each poem amazed me every time, and continues to remind me that any two things can connect, find a place of shared life, and from that place shed light on something that is real. These little poems, then, in some ways, are like sacraments of Jesus' beatitude where He said, "Blessed are the peacemakers, for they shall be called children of God." These poems, in some sense my children, are doing in my world what I, as God's child, am to be doing in His world: bring together the odd and the at-odds, the strange and the estranged, and in the meeting to see forged something new and whole and bright.

The Bee Keeper to the Heart Surgeon

The comb is full of honey.
Such sweetness settling
after ceaseless effort.

When the plaque has narrowed
the way in and out,
just before the jam,

I wonder if you find
the compilation waxing
the tired walls a kind

of beauty? Testament
to hard work and sac-
rifice gathered up,

waving little children
lining the parade,
goodbyes thick with love?

The Librarian to the Lion Tamer

Tech has the whip,
and I am jumping through
hot hoop after hoop.

It won't be long now
until these thick dark
corridors I tend,

dangerous with old pages
yellowing, smelling of must,
cool between fingers,

are captured behind
screens and called up
to do tricks at the push

of a button, torn
out of their borders, dragged
from their leaved bush.

The Quadriplegic to the Sous Chef

You look tired after
another twelve hour shift
of making the head chef

look good. He doesn't know,
does he, what he has?
You are his hands and feet

bringing his cuisine
to life in the cramped
but clean Babel kitchen,

flurry of intricate fingers
over steam and spigot.
Though his name in town

is known, still you know
the simple, exquisite pleasure
of laying the garnish down.

The Plastic Surgeon to the Weatherman

We are not fated to face
the encroaching autumn chill
just because you say

it comes this way. We skirt
its path with knife and suction.
We dare see undone

the surest forecast by
ducking nature's blast
before the storm has passed.

Cumulus breasts are ours
to command. Ours to deny
at the first skiff of snow

the winter of our days,
the gathering of the wrinkles,
the chilblains of the nose.

The Ballerina to the Logger

The splitting whine of your chain
saw slices the cool
morning air and just

as easily swims through
the dark sullen trunk,
spitting a spray of splinter

and stops. The teetering
tree cracks a whimper,
its terrible plié,

then up on its pointed toe,
gracefully twirling its last
pirouette with precision,

falls through the arms
of its feckless friends
into final position.

The Porn Film Director to the Tomato Farmer

I traffic in hunger as you,
hauling into the market
cages what customers crave

and will pay for, fruit
with tight skin over soft flesh.
You say ugly ones

are better, those that easily
crack and split, like lips,
on the tumbling ride

from field to table. I
say start with pretty
and tough, then throw them back

after the cameras have sucked
them blank, bled all blushing
red to withered black.

The Arborist to the Soccer Mom

Each one has a Latin
name which I cannot
pronounce as I should.

But I know how to grow them--
good soil, sun and shade,
deft with the pruning blade,

though I cannot predict
all the coming contours--
which limbs will need attention

when and where to cut--
until the time's at hand
on the way to tall,

always watching, tense
at sudden sprints of wind,
at each inevitable fall.

The Florist to the Telemarketer

You arrange your
words so carefully,
showing off the best

first, the bright colors
and dazzling scent
of whatever it is

you are pedaling. I know
most people hang up.
In between the calls

be sure to take a water
break. Too much
rejection, like direct sun,

can wither the tender skin
your soul is wrapped up in
and cause black spot infection.

The Fetus to the Crane Operator

My little heart leaps
when I think of the joy
of the iron girders

long stacked in the dark
alley swinging free
underneath your arm--

long, strong and steady--
rising up, up
into the startling sunlight

above the building rims
toward their high home
in the skeleton cage,

far now from the menacing
forklift with its skewers
skulking in the shade.

The Parole Officer to the Meter Reader

Can you recall the kilowatt
usage of each house
from its previous month

as you approach the read,
wondering if you will see
splurge or patient restraint?

And what is it you wish
for? To see the out-
of-control spinning,

or the measured pace
of those who've learned their lesson,
though that be a bore,

like a storm late turning
away from the boarded
up deserted shore?

The Mathematician to the Crab Fisherman

It doesn't add up:
death rate off the chart;
working season short;

declining annual catch;
Just the weight of the cages
concave over raging

polar ocean swells
should surface second thoughts.
Yet you are clamoring

your grubby best to grab
a crabbing spot on one
of the few boats leaving shore,

the quota keeping count,
and you alive as sure
as two and two are four.

The English Professor to the Exterminator

Do you dream of roaches
taking their revenge--
pouring from the walls

in waterfalls of quiver?
Their plot hatched in the winter,
an epic infestation

where the wasps and weevils
heed the Great Eye's summons
for a hero to lead them out--

a Faustian wolf spider
devil-pact empowered
and for greatness bound

from his burrow rising
like remorseless Aaron the Moor
upraised from the ground.

The Hair Stylist to the Highway Patrolman

The license on my wall
testifies that I
am to make beautiful

the messes that I meet.
That keeps me going.
Were I only to snip

the snarled and wash away
the oil and grime and quit
before the shaping, I

would despair. For hair
will insist on breaking
outside the boundaries set,

drunk on its freedom to frazzle,
reckless in the thrill of
fleeing the barrette.

The Chimney Sweep to the Wedding Planner

A century ago naked
young boys climbed into
the dark narrow flues

and shimmied upward on
calloused elbows and knees
knocking loose the soot.

Do you remind them--
after choosing music,
colors, flowers, cake--

of the climb that awaits,
the turns in the dark,
crusted creosote

fires waiting to happen,
save the dirty work
of brush stroke after stroke?

The Stockbroker to the Truck Driver

As you pass slowly
the even slower truck
and watch the growing line

of impatient cars
lengthening behind,
do you take interest

in the building tension?
Or after all these years
is the risk of moving

over over-rated?
The little people will surely
soon resume and then some,

and finally make it home
despite the irritation
of some lost momentum.

The Preacher to the Toll Booth Attendant

Your Sunday to greet
the gummed line of glum
faces crawling by

handing over some
bills or coins to pay
the toll to cross the bridge.

They are feeling robbed,
resenting you, and you
just doing your joyless job

managing the ransom
from the necessary traveler.
How different it would be

if you were bearing news
the day had finally come
that they could pass for free.

The Marxist-Leninist to the Dentist

There are rebels in the row
refusing the line, to which
the patient work of wires

and cement will attend.
Only rogues revel in
riding lone the chariot,

threatening to unravel
the rising proletariat.
What foments in the canal

that breeds breaking rank
must be rooted out,
nerve replaced by rubber,

crowning in porcelain
submission that wayward
artist and his lover.

The Animal Control Officer to the Opera Singer

The coyote raids
on suburban streets
are not so subtle

anymore, the way
they snatch cats
off sleepy porches

in brazen acts, howling
shrill cries over the
still audience of night,

impossible vocalizations
of hunger and lust, hunters
unchallenged and bored,

dangling prey like Carmen
playing with Don Jose
white-knuckling his sword.

The Panhandler to the Auto Mechanic

There are plenty of people
who patently think to fix
what is wrong with me,

eschewing the jangle of coins
while generous with advice,
hoisting up the hood

of my disheveled life
to point out oil leaks,
how corroded cables should

be replaced, how pistons
turn the resistant crank
at the lash of sparks,

and they the beneficent fuel,
combusting wise to force
my stuck gear out of park.

The Plumber to the Shoe Salesman

Do you know the world
is leaking? Can't you tell it
by the squeaking of

your tennis shoes upon
the hardwood floors that will
be ruined by this wet?

I cannot keep up.
If I move faster
I arrive at next

before the last is fixed
and find the following flood
swallowing up my span.

Have you waders that float?
I need to walk on water
or find someone who can.

The Scuba Diver to the Advertising Executive

Things work different down
here in the deep and dark
where eyes are larger

for lack of light
in the murky rocking
underworld of sea.

You know when they see
without knowing they see
they will think your thoughts

theirs, instincts borne
freely on the air
without prompt or proctor,

all while your low
chthonic cadence drums
from Davey Jones' locker.

The Phlebotomist to the Solar Panel Installer

From the heaven-mirroring
slanted surfaces on
my roof into my room

flows life for plug and bulb.
You need not puncture sky
to draw out the currents

coursing unseen within
it (feeding the plant
and wrapping warm the lizard)

as I must, after blood,
the vein. How charming Helios
rides dark the cavernous

space invisible
but dyes alarmingly red
on reaching our air at dusk!

The Mortician to the Fashion Magazine Editor

I apply the base
thick and evenly to
hide the sunken blotches

death has left behind.
A touch of blush and eye-
liner accent. He

is dressed in double-breasted
wool, with folded hands,
cool on coffin silk.

You would think him sleeping,
as I think your girls
wide awake and eager

to remain one air-
brushed step ahead
of their shadowy Reaper.

The Old Woman to the Grocery Clerk

I can hardly believe
how the years have passed
through my juggling hands

leaving wrinkles and lists
of scrawled gratefuls
and regrets, mixed

together most of the time,
frozen with the fresh.
How the unexpected

often snuck up on
unsuspecting sorrow
and angled it precise

enough to barely miss
the red eye registering
the undiscounted price.

The Secularist to God

You have had your time
big in the mind of man.
Can't you see it's right

to retire now
that we have things
so obviously in hand?

You were better fit
for superstitious days
when barbarism ruled,

before we understood
we could explain it all
without you in the mix.

.

Look how high we've come,
and to what clouds we'll go,
what quality these bricks.

God to the Secularist

It's getting late and I
see you have not quite
figured out how

to elude the stalking past.
Maddening, isn't it?
All this talk of promise

and progress only to find
your world full of words
hopelessly unhinged from

what the dawn reveals,
what sits in the road,
what waits in the dark

impervious to all
your passionate notions
of how things really are.

Jeff Reed serves on the Lead Pastor Team of Hillside Covenant Church in Walnut Creek, CA. He is the author of many books including *Kore on the Trail of the Tree Keepers, Lamentation of Swans, In Search of J. Morton Allen,* and *Mene Tekel.* He lives in Orinda, CA with his wife Susan. You can follow his poetry blog at www.windinthereeds.com

www.ingramcontent.com/pod-product-compliance
Lightning Source LLC
Chambersburg PA
CBHW031618040426

42452CB00006B/579

9 780989 738903